From Healing to Wholeness

A Christian Perspective on Emotional and Mental Wellness

Ebony Hudson

ISBN 978-1-63903-716-2 (paperback)
ISBN 978-1-63903-717-9 (digital)

Copyright © 2021 by Ebony Hudson

All rights reserved. No part of this publication may be reproduced, distributed, or transmitted in any form or by any means, including photocopying, recording, or other electronic or mechanical methods without the prior written permission of the publisher. For permission requests, solicit the publisher via the address below.

Christian Faith Publishing, Inc.
832 Park Avenue
Meadville, PA 16335
www.christianfaithpublishing.com

All the biblical verses in this book are cited from the King James Version of the Bible unless otherwise noted.

Printed in the United States of America

Contents

Chapter 1: The Importance of Wellness 5
Chapter 2: Nothing New under the Sun 23
Chapter 3: The Truth about Your Identity 44
Chapter 4: The Art of Self-Encouragement 58
Chapter 5: A Bright Future 68

Chapter 1

THE IMPORTANCE OF WELLNESS

In Luke 17:11–19, we read the story of the ten men who had leprosy and cried out to Jesus for healing. In the process of their obedience in following Jesus's instructions to go to the priests, they were healed. However, there was one leper who, after realizing that he was healed from the disease, returned to Jesus and gave Him praise and gratitude. In verse 19, Jesus is recorded as saying, "Arise, go thy way: thy faith hath made thee whole." In reading that passage of scripture, I have always focused on the fact that ten were healed, and only one came back to thank Jesus. As I was studying the passage again recently, verse 19 stuck out to me. I thought to myself, the man was already healed, yet Jesus told him the second time that he was made whole. Is it possible to be healed and not whole? Is it possible to be well in one or two areas of our lives and yet not whole? Does it really matter if I'm "whole"? Couldn't the one leper just be happy that he was healed? Why did he have to turn back? Do I need to turn back? What does wholeness look like?

A familiar scripture in the Bible is 3 John 1:2, which reads, "Beloved, I wish above all things that thou mayest prosper and be in health, even as thy soul prosper." So I can be prosperous in business, finances, and career as well as be healthy (not just physically and mentally but emotionally as well) and have my soul right with God; that sounds like wholeness! In my work as a clinical social worker, I have been trained to look at the whole person, the systems that impact that person, and to help them achieve wellness, not only in the area that they are seeking help with, but also recognizing that there are other areas that they need to address in order to have well-rounded wellness or wholeness. As a Christian, I am called to not only read the Bible but also to live the Bible, and if it says I can be healed and made whole, I am striving to be both healed and made whole. Wholeness does refer to all areas of life—physical, spiritual, financial, emotional, mental, and social. However, for purposes of this book, I am focusing on emotional and mental health; and although wholeness is important for every individual, regardless of religious beliefs, I am focusing on this topic from a Christian perspective.

One of the ways in which we attempt to determine how well we are doing is by determining if we are "normal." We ask such questions as, Am I normal? Is my family normal? Are my relationships normal? Who is normal? What is normal? These are age-old questions that we all ask ourselves at some time or another. In a society where celebrities, social media, and political agendas determine "the norm," it is a question whose answer is ever-changing. The better question is "Does normal really exist?" The fact is that what is normal for one person is not, and cannot be, normal for another, just as the areas that we need healing are based on our individual needs. What is normal for each of us changes, so our sense of normal is very fluid. Ecclesiastes 3:1 (KJV) says, "To everything there is a season, and a time to every purpose under the heaven." As with nature, our lives go through different seasons, usually a lot faster than the four seasons.

Let's look at "normal" from the natural and spiritual perspectives. I believe that in order to maintain good mental health, we must stop asking and wondering if we are normal. That does not mean to suggest that some of the symptoms we experience, both physically and mentally, are not abnormal, therefore requiring professional attention, treatment, and/or preventative measures. One of the reasons it is not helpful to focus on the question of normality is because it is always changing, and if you try to keep up with all the changes as established by society, it can produce anxiety and feelings of insecurity and hopelessness, which are enemies of healing and wholeness.

Normal does, and should, include many societal norms. Obeying laws, observing personal space, using inside and outside voices appropriately, wearing clothes in public, and good hygiene are just a few examples of what we would consider a societal norm. What is a normal lifestyle for us becomes a problem when it has a negative effect on us physically, mentally, spiritually, financially, etc. It also becomes a problem for us when it negatively affects our family, community, or society at large. When we experience these negative consequences in our lives, we seek healing in that area and begin the journey to wholeness.

Have you ever watched a child try to shove an object of one shape into an object of another shape and become increasingly frustrated because it doesn't fit? In some ways, this is what we do when it comes to discussing normal. If we consider our lives before some event and/or passage of time as a circle shape and our current life as a triangle shape, many of us become like the child trying to force the circle into the triangle and become increasingly frustrated when it doesn't fit. For the child, frustration can be observed in the form of temper tantrums, throwing objects, and/or crying. For adults, the frustration can be observed as depression, anxiety, suicidal ideations, and other emotional problems. We must learn that when life changes our shape, we must come to terms with its new shape or take appropriate steps to changing into what we want our normal to look like, without obsessing about what it used to be since we cannot go back in time. You are allowed to grieve over your past normal, but please don't live in your past as that can have negative ramifications on your present and future.

Taking care of our physical bodies is so important to our mental health and well-being; it is important to our spiritual health as well. When I worked as a social worker on an inpatient mental health unit and we had someone admitted with such diagnoses as depression, suicidal thoughts, and psychosis, with no previous history, the first thing the doctor would do is a medical workup. They wanted to make sure that the presenting mental health symptoms were not due to some underlying medical issue. We know just from watching the commercials that many medications can have side effects that resemble minor and/or major mental health symptoms. How well do you take care of yourself physically? How much sleep do you get and is it a restful sleep? How balanced is your diet? Do you exercise? And does God really care about the answers to these questions? *Yes!*

In addition to 3 John 1:2, 1 Corinthians 6:19–20 states, "What? know ye not that your body is the temple of the Holy Ghost which is in you, which ye have of God, and ye are not your own? For ye are brought with a price: therefore glorify God in your body, and in your spirit, which are God's." Take care of *you*. I know that's easier said than done since for many of us, it is easier and more natural to put others first. Many people even feel a sense of guilt for taking care of themselves as it seems selfish and arrogant, but it is of vital importance. My intention is not to tell you what to eat, how much to exercise, or what kind of mattress and pillow you should sleep on; but I would suggest speaking with your medical personnel on ways in which you can achieve and maintain a healthy lifestyle. If you are suddenly experiencing mental health symptoms and difficulties coping with life and everyday occurrences, I would recommend seeking professional help. Sometimes, it may be due to something as simple as medicines or medication interactions. At other times, your medical professional may recommend counseling, group therapy, and/or support groups. Treat your body as the temple God says it is.

I am a big proponent of relaxation techniques and taking even five to ten minutes a day to clear our minds of the busyness of the day. As a Christian, I believe the best relaxation techniques are those that bring our mind back to the Prince of Peace, one of His names (and character traits) as listed in Isaiah 9:6–7. John 14:27 says, "Peace I leave with you, my peace I give unto you; not as the world giveth give I unto you. Let not your heart be troubled, neither let it be afraid." The following is a brief relaxation technique I use, and it can be adapted to better suit each individual. The purpose is more important than the process. Find a technique that works best for you.

Get into a very comfortable position, close your eyes, and make sure the environment is quiet with no distractions. Visualize yourself on your favorite beach. See the ocean, the waves, hear the movement of the water, and feel the warm sand on your feet. Now visualize that Jesus is sitting next to you, and lay your head on His shoulder, but don't speak. Let the cares of the world diminish as the reality sets in that you are leaning on the King of kings, the Lord of lords, the Prince of Peace, the Great I Am, He who rose from the dead with *all* power in His hands, the all-knowing, all-wise God. There is no need to tell Him all your problems for He already knows, and His soft response in your ear is John 14:27 or Jeremiah 29:11–13, "For I know the thoughts that I think toward you, saith the Lord, thoughts of peace, and not of evil…and ye shall seek me, and find me, when you shall search for me with all your heart."

Input your favorite scripture or one that you find encouraging and offers you hope. I identified and used two scriptures that I find encouraging because they speak about peace, but you may find other scriptures that minister to you. Now go and guard your temple!

When He says He wishes above all things that we prosper and be in health even as our soul prospers, that includes our mental health. James 1:8 says "A double minded man is unstable in all his ways." Philippians 4:6–7 says:

> Be careful (or anxious) for nothing; but in everything by prayer and supplication with thanksgiving let your requests be made known unto God.
> And the peace of God that passeth all understanding shall keep your hearts and minds through Christ Jesus.

God is concerned about our mental health, the state of our mind. The Prince of Peace wants us to obtain peace and walk in that peace daily. The stresses of life can sometimes cause us to feel as though we are "losing our minds." We can have so much in our mind that we cannot concentrate on even simple tasks. We may become irritable, argumentative, and insecure, with negative and self-defeating thoughts taking up permanent residence in our mind. Our minds can become a runaway train of negative thinking, where one negative thought produces another and another and before you know it—you feel sad, depressed, anxious, weak, and defeated. And you may not have even gotten out of bed; you are just lying there *thinking*. Many times, we are our own worst enemy. The worst place many of us can find ourselves is alone with our thoughts.

Let's look at what the scriptures say about our thoughts and changing our mindset in order to maintain good mental health and peace of mind.

> Commit thy works unto the LORD, and thy thoughts shall be established. (Proverbs 16:3)

> For the word of God is quick, and powerful, and sharper than any twoedged sword, piercing even to the dividing asunder of soul and spirit, and of the joints and marrow, and is a discerner of the thoughts and intents of the heart. (Hebrews 4:12)

Solutions are found in Romans 7:14–25, which concludes Paul stating, "I thank God through Jesus Christ our

Lord. So then with the mind I myself serve the law of God; but with the flesh the law of sin."

> That ye be not soon shaken in mind, or be troubled, neither by spirit, nor by word, nor by letter as from us, as that the day of Christ is at hand. (2 Thessalonians 2:2)

> Wherefore gird up the loins of your mind, be sober, and hope to the end for the grace that is to be brought unto you at the revelation of Jesus Christ. (1 Peter 1:13)

We must put on the mind of Christ in order to maintain peace in our own minds. I can hear you say, *Easier said than done!* My reply: Who said it would be easy?

When we are commanded to love our neighbor as ourselves, is that easy? The command to pay tithes and offerings—is that easy? The price that Jesus paid so that we could become Christians—was that easy? We must put in the work if we want the reward.

So what are some practical ways in which we can put on the mind of Christ and decrease a negative mindset, which can lead to depression, anxiety, suicidal thoughts, physical illness, and other consequences that affect good mental health and peace of mind? Let me start with what *not* to do. *Do not* focus on *not* focusing on negative thoughts. If I told you whatever you do, *do not* think about ice cream; *do not* think about vanilla, strawberry, chocolate, or my favorite, rocky road. *Do not* think about it on a waffle cone with rainbow sprinkles. I don't know about you, but for most people, the thing they would be thinking about is *ice cream*.

You also have to be careful when people say "Just think positive thoughts." Well, if it was that easy, we wouldn't be where we are, locked into a negative mindset. A better solution to me is what I call thought substitution. When I ran group therapy and was trying to help individuals obtain and maintain healthy coping skills, I would have them visualize a cabinet with food. The current food in the cabinet is their negative coping skills. We cannot expect them to take out all the negative coping skills and leave the cabinet bare. Why not? Because human nature is to go back to what we know. If the cabinet is empty, we are going to refill it with the things we just took out; therefore, you have to substitute what was taken out with something else so that when the person opens the cabinet to take out a coping skill, it is as full, or fuller, than before, just with positive and healthy substitutions.

That's what we have to do with our thought process and mindset. Begin to substitute those negative thoughts with positive and godly substitutions. This does not mean that you deny your responsibilities or circumstances, but that you have a constructive mindset to deal with those circumstances. Remember that you are not alone in life and have a Father who knows the number of the very hairs on your head; certainly He is concerned, willing, and able to help with "the issues of life." The fact that we have to deal with life on life's terms does not mean that we forget we serve a God who can change life's terms.

Matthew 8:27 recalls the disciples when Jesus spoke to a storm. They said, "What manner of man is this, that even the winds and the waves obey Him!" If you can find positive thoughts or sayings as your substitutions, go for it; but if not, open the Bible and find scriptures that encourage you and speak to your situation. I believe that as you do this, the Holy Spirit will provide more positive thoughts until your cup runneth over and your mind is at peace. Jeremiah 29:13 states, "And ye shall seek me, and find me, when ye shall search for me with all your heart." Seek Him in the scriptures, and you will find Him. Put in the effort, and you will see a great reward.

1 Peter 2:9 says that "ye are a chosen generation, a royal priesthood, a holy nation, a peculiar people; that ye should shew forth the praises of him who hath called you out of darkness into his marvelous light." As Christians, our normal lifestyle must be one that pleases Him, who brought us out of darkness into the light. Matthew 7:20 says, "By their fruits ye shall know them." The problem is that the norms of society and the norms of a holy lifestyle usually don't coincide with one another and are more often in opposition. 1 Corinthians 1:25–28 speaks of how the foolishness of God is still wiser than men. He does not adjust His requirements for holy living based on the latest trend or popularity poll.

Now let's discuss normal from a spiritual perspective. I was recently reading the story of Elijah in 1 Kings 18:21–40, in which the prophet challenges the prophets of Baal to see who was the true God. The challenge was to place a bull on the altar but put no fire under it. The prophets of Baal would pray to their God to put a fire under their sacrifice, and Elijah would pray to the God of heaven to put fire under his sacrifice. Nothing happened when the prophets of Baal prayed. Before Elijah prayed to the Lord in verses 33–35, he instructed that water be put on the sacrifice to the point in which verse 35 says, "And the water ran about the altar; and he filled the trench also with water." When Elijah prayed to the Lord, verse 38 says, "Then the fire of the Lord fell, and consumed the burnt sacrifice, and the wood, and the stones, and the dust, and licked up the water that was in the trench." When we talk about dealing with life from a spiritual perspective, we are talking about the need for the fire of God. When we feel like the bull on the altar and life is pouring on problem after problem, issue after issue until we feel overwhelmed and it's spilling over into other areas of our lives, we need the fire of God. Not to consume us on the outside but consume us on the inside until we feel empowered to continue going from faith to faith and focusing on things eternal, not being overwhelmed by things of the earth.

One of the hardest scriptures to follow when we feel overwhelmed, helpless, and hopeless is Colossians 3:2: "Set your affections on things above, not on things on the earth." I can hear your response again: "Easier said than done." I agree, but if the Lord commanded it, aren't we commanded to obey? We are tempted to focus on our circumstances and situations, tempted to give in to whatever emotions we have at any given moment, even if those emotions are unhealthy. It is so easy to give in to these temptations, however, 1 Corinthians 10:13 says, "There hath no temptation taken you but such as is common to man: "but God" is faithful, who will not suffer you to be tempted above that ye are able; but will with the temptation also make a way to escape, that ye may be able to bear it." My interpretation of that scripture is that it's normal to want to focus on everyday problems that we can see, touch, and feel, "but God" says that it is possible for us to not let these things overtake us. This takes practice and it is hard work, but it is part of the Christian experience—to be able to keep our eyes on Christ while living in a natural world that puts demands on us to keep our eyes on everything else. I think of it as being similar to driving a car through a very scenic area, we want to focus on the beauty around us, yet we know that we must also keep our eyes on the road in order to survive the journey.

This life is a journey, and we should not only want to survive it but enjoy it. We want to ride through it, aware of all the sights, sounds, and experiences around us while never taking our eyes off the road. What is the road? Christ is the road. John 14:6 says, "Jesus saith unto him, I am the way, the truth, and the life." It takes practice to keep your eyes on the road, and as the saying goes, "practice makes perfect." In order to keep our eyes on Christ, I believe we have to keep our focus on the Word of God, prayer, and praise. I cannot emphasize strongly enough the importance of the Word of God in our daily life in order to maintain wellness in all areas of life. Jesus himself tells us in Luke 4:4: "It is written, that man shall not live by bread alone, but by every word of God." The greatest challenge is finding time to get in the Word and to read the Bible in a way that it transforms us from the inside out.

One of the most important ways in which to include the Word of God on a constant basis is to develop a personal strategy. Develop a plan that works for you and your schedule. One mistake many of us make is to try to force Bible study time into our daily schedule, like trying to fit a size eight body into size zero jeans. When we do this, the result is unproductive and ineffective Bible study—we read with little to no comprehension, we fall asleep or spend time daydreaming, we feel guilty that we have prioritized other things above our Bible study, we make promises to do better the next day, week, month, etc., and the cycle continues. Personal Bible study has to be like clothes shopping; you have to find what fits you.

For me personally, I had to try several strategies until I found one that works for me and my busy lifestyle. And please give the Bible the respect it is due. It is not just another good book; it is the living word of the living God and should be treated and studied as such. Second Timothy 3:16–17 tells us that "all scripture is given by inspiration of God, and is profitable for doctrine, for reproof, for correction, for instruction in righteousness: That the man of God may be perfect, thoroughly furnished unto all good works." When we realize that the Word of God is living and can speak to every circumstance of life, we desire to spend as much time in it as possible. Psalm 1:1–3 reminds us:

> Blessed is the man that walketh not in the counsel of the ungodly, nor standeth in the way of sinners, nor sitteth in the seat of the scornful. But his delight is in the law of the Lord; and in his law does he meditate day and night. And he shall be like a tree planted by the rivers of water, that bringeth forth his fruit in his season.

Lastly, I highly recommend Bible study guides that clearly explain what the book, chapter, and/or verse is talking about, including historical background and geographical information. The Bible is so much more powerful when we have an understanding of what it is saying, and how we can apply the Word to our current everyday life. I have recently started purchasing Bible study notes for every book of the Bible and cannot begin to tell you how alive the Word has become, with a full and much better understanding of scriptures that I have heard, read, and reread for years.

Another major aspect of our spiritual well-being is prayer. Prayer has been described as open and honest communication with God. The Bible is full of examples of men and women who prayed, including Jesus. There is power in prayer, and you must believe that in order to see its effect in your life and on your well-being. Prayer is so powerful. 2 Chronicles 7:14 states that "if my people, which are called by name, will humble themselves, and pray, and seek my face, and turn from their wicked ways: then will I hear from heaven and will forgive their sin, and will heal their land." We have to continually pray the will of God, the word of God, and the way of God.

There are many examples of the power of prayer in the Bible, but I want to look at the story of King Hezekiah in 2 Kings 20. I am going to paraphrase, but I encourage you to read the whole chapter as part of your Bible study of the books of 1 and 2 Kings. Verse 1 tells us that King Hezekiah was "sick unto death" and the prophet Isaiah informed him that he was going to die. Verse 2 tells us that Hezekiah "turned his face to the wall and prayed unto the Lord." As we continue to read, we find that the Lord was so moved by Hezekiah's prayer that before Isaiah was out of the building, the Lord told him go back again and tell Hezekiah: "I have heard thy prayer, I have seen thy tears: behold I will heal thee…and I will add unto thy days fifteen years."

I do not know how that story will impact your life, but it has had a great impact on mine, and I am sure multitudes of believers throughout history. The fact that the prayer of one human being—not a divine being, not an angel, not even a perfect person, but a normal human being like you and I—could move the God of all creation in a way that causes a divine change of plans is both powerful and encouraging. Life had set the king on a course of sickness and death; and this course was confirmed by God through the prophet. But with heavy heart and tear-filled eyes, the king prayed to the only person who has the power to both spiritually and naturally change the course of life itself.

What course does life have you on? What are your issues, struggles, diagnoses, anxieties, and addictions that have you on an unfavorable, destructive, and unwanted course? Only you know the answer to those questions, and they may be answers that only you and God know. So if the answers to those questions are the problem, what is the solution? The solution is prayer to the Lord of all creation, the only one who has the power to literally change the course of your life. It makes me think of train tracks and how, when a train needs to change tracks, a switch is hit to change the direction of the track, which in turn changes the direction of the train. Prayer is the key to letting God know our train is heading in a direction that is off course, and we need Him to flip the switch. And remember that He knows *all*, so do not be afraid to confess your sins, issues, addictions, and anxieties with Him.

Many times, He is waiting for our confession and repentance before He takes action. Matthew 7:7 instructs us to "ask, and it shall be given; seek, and ye shall find; knock, and it shall be opened unto you." We want God to do His part in fixing our lives, but are we willing to do our part of asking, seeking, and knocking? 1 Thessalonians 5:17 tells us to pray without ceasing. There should always be a prayer in our heart, even if just a prayer of thanksgiving and gratitude. One of the most important instructions in regard to praying is found in Mark 11:24: "What things soever you desire, when you pray, believe that you receive them, and you shall have them."

If you pray and don't believe that your prayers can or will be answered, your prayers are ineffective and powerless. Hebrews 11 tells us that faith is "the substance of things hoped for, the evidence of things not seen." Thinking back on the train analogy, imagine if every train conductor started the journey not believing that any of the switches would be turned on, and he/she would never be able to change course and get to the designated destination. I do not think we would have many successful or effective train conductors. Let's have a prayer life built on strong faith; one in which our strong prayer life builds upon our strong faith, and our strong faith builds up a strong prayer life. Believe that not only *can* God do it, but that He *will* do it; and the course of our life will be divinely set and will reflect the will of God, the word of God, and the way of God.

Another aspect of our spiritual life that must become normal is praise and having an attitude of gratitude. Psalm 150:6 states, "Let everything that hath breath praise the LORD. Praise ye the LORD." In the midst of life circumstances, both good and bad, we must practice praise. The Bible teaches the Christian in Colossians 3:2 to "set your affections on things above, not on things on the earth." Is it easy to find anything praiseworthy when we are depressed, anxious, and dealing with the stressors of life? *Absolutely not!* Whether we are aware of it or not, we do fake it until we make it at times. This is why individuals can commit suicide, and those around them had no idea of their level of depression and feelings of hopelessness.

We may have difficulties at home yet bring no evidence of such into our workplace, churches, and/or outside relationships. In the same manner that we put aside other issues in order to focus on the task at hand, we must force ourselves to do the same in order to focus on the praise at hand. If you do not know where to start, I encourage you to read the book of Psalms. Since it instructs everything that has breath to praise the Lord, you can start by saying thank you for breath. Where there is breath, there is hope. I desire for people reading this book to have hope. When we find hope in nothing else, the Lord wants to be our hope. Psalm 71:14 says, "But I will hope continually and yet praise thee more and more." Romans 12:12 says, "Rejoicing in hope, patient in tribulation, continuing instant in prayer."

I wish hope was something we could bottle up and hand out as needed. I believe that hopelessness is one of the worst emotions we can ever experience. The question then becomes, How does praise change this emotion? First, praise and an attitude of gratitude force us to think about something else. If we are forced to think about something else, that means there is something else to think about. Let's think about hopelessness in terms of a train. One car alone does not make a train too heavy or too long, but when you continue to add on train cars, it becomes harder to pull. When we ruminate about problems, situations, and/or emotions, we become so drained by the length and weight that we feel hopeless. Praise allows us to stop connecting train cars of negativity and self-defeat in order to decrease the weight of the world on our shoulders.

Second, it forces us to set our affections on things above and on the *all-powerful* God. I believe that God is *all-powerful* and can do anything, including miracles. I make no apologies for this belief and when I discuss praise, it is with this belief system in mind. We are offering up praise and thanksgiving to the only one who can truly change our situation and our mindset. If we believe in the greatness of our God when compared to whatever we are going through, hopelessness has to decrease. If we take the largest city in the world and compare it to the whole planet, even it looks very small. It becomes not about the size of my problem but the size of my God.

Third, when we praise and are thankful for past accomplishments, it builds faith. The continued building of faith decreases hopelessness. Despite what we may feel in the moment, all of us have past successes and accomplishments. For many people, their greatest accomplishment is survival; their ability to have survived the hell they have been through. Do not ever minimize your successes and accomplishments, including survival, as these are necessary steppingstones on your faith walk and life journey. During difficult times in my own life, I have praised and thanked God off just one verse found in Romans 8:18: "For I reckon that the sufferings of this present time are not worthy to be compared with the glory which shall be revealed in us." I personalize this verse for myself to mean that the things I am going through right now are nothing when compared to what the Lord is going to do in and through me. Find your own praiseworthy scripture, and personalize it for yourself.

Chapter 2

NOTHING NEW UNDER THE SUN

Various myths exist in relation to Christians and mental health, including that Christians do not and should not get depressed, suicidal, or suffer with anxiety. Some people believe Christians should not seek counseling while others feel that mental and emotional problems are representative of an individual's relationship with the Lord. None of the above beliefs are true. Christians experience life just as anyone else; we just have a hope that relies on a power higher than ourselves. Let's look at individuals in the Bible who also experienced life stressors and the impact it had on their mental health.

We love to hear about David's experience in 1 Chronicles 15:25–29 when he is so happy about the return of the Ark of the Covenant that he dances so much that even his wife is embarrassed. We do not like to hear as much about his depression and despair and his feelings of fear that, at its worst, caused him to hide in caves. Many of the chapters and scriptures of Psalms show us David's pleas with the Lord for help in his despair. Just one example in Psalms 28:1–2 (NIV), where David prays: "To you Lord I call; you are my rock, do not turn a deaf ear to me. For if you remain silent, I will be like those who go down to the pit. Hear my cry for mercy as I call to you for help."

When we look at some of the Old Testament prophets, many of them exhibit what we would diagnose today as anxiety and depression. For most, the sheer magnitude of what God was calling them to do was anxiety producing. One such prophet we find in Habakkuk 1:1–3 (KJV): "The burden which Habakkuk the prophet did see. O Lord, how long shall I cry, and thou wilt not hear! Even cry unto thee of violence and thou wilt not save! Why dost thou shew me iniquity and cause me to behold grievance?"

If a man who is identified as a man after God's own heart and the prophets God called to relay his messages on earth can experience fear, depression, anxiety, and despair, why is it strange to believe that Christians today cannot experience the same? While in an earthly body, even Jesus experienced emotions of anger (remember when he flipped that table over in the temple) and sadness as explained in the shortest verse in the Bible, John 11:35 (KJV): "Jesus wept." Don't feel alone when experiencing mental and emotional problems. Christianity does not guard us from experiencing negative emotions and mental health issues, but it certainly gives us a foundation to step on in our despair as well as an unmovable and unshakable force to hold onto as the journey of life continues, with both the good and the bad, the positive and the negative, all the steps forward, and even the steps back.

Although there are a multitude of mental health diagnoses, I want to focus on two of the more prevalent and common ones: depression and anxiety. There are various types of depression, however, the general DSM-5 criteria for depression include a depressed mood most of the day, nearly every day; significant diminished interest or pleasure in all, or almost all, activities most of the day, nearly every day; significant weight loss when not dieting or weight gain; or a decrease/increase in appetite nearly every day. Obviously, a person can feel sad without being depressed, but continued feelings of sadness, with no improvement or positive outlet and coping skills, can lead to depression. A severe case of depression and hopelessness can lead to suicidal thoughts.

Many times, what hinders people from discussing and seeking help for their feelings of depression is the belief that they are alone, weak, unable to have happiness in their life, or will be outed as a person with a mental illness. So right now, I want to confirm and state emphatically that *you are not alone, you are not weak, you can experience happiness in your life*, and being diagnosed with a mental health issue at some point in your life *does not identify who you are or who you will be*. In Ecclesiastes 1:9, it states, "The thing that hath been, it is that which shall be; and that which is done is that which shall be done: and there is no new thing under the sun." There is nothing new under the sun, which means depression is not new. If you experience feelings of depression, you are not the first and, unfortunately, you will not be the last person to experience such feelings. Also, because there is nothing new under the sun, feelings of depression do not come as a shock or surprise to God. We have already read that many people in the Bible had to deal with their own feelings of depression during life's journey, and they were still used for great accomplishments that we talk about centuries later.

So what are some practical steps to dealing with depression? There are hundreds, possibly thousands, of books written in regard to answering this question; and in today's society of "there's an app for that," there are multiple apps to help identify possible solutions as well. However, I want to address four practical steps that I believe can help address feelings of depression, and in turn, hopefully decrease any thoughts of suicide. The steps are the following: (1) identify the root cause(s), (2) take appropriate steps to work through the root causes, (3) define and visualize life with reduced or no depression, and (4) keep your guard up.

Step 1 is identifying the root cause(s) that impact depression. I remember when I wanted to get rid of a large bush that blocked the window and attracted a large number of flies in front of my first new house. When I started calling around to various companies that could cut down the tree, they asked if I would also pay to have the roots dug up. As a single female who wasn't making a lot of money and now had all the expenses of a new home, I wanted to take the cheap way out and just pay to have the bush cut. However, in speaking to coworkers, they disagreed with my thought process and told me that if I don't like the bush and don't want it to return, I have to be willing to pay extra to have the stumps and roots totally removed. Well, in being completely honest with you, I didn't want to spend the money, so the stump and roots stayed for a while until season after season, the bush kept growing and attracting those same annoying flies, so I had to do what I was told in the beginning: spend the money and have it all removed.

In dealing with depression and the negative consequences we have in our lives, we have to get to the root cause(s). I believe that is one of the great benefits of therapy—a neutral person who helps to identify those areas that may seem impossible for you to identify on your own. Some people are able to easily identify root causes while other causes are buried so deep the task feels almost impossible. And let me be clear: I do believe that some root causes are biological and require some form of medication, administered by a psychiatrist or other medical personnel. However, even if the cause is biological and medication is prescribed, there are other root causes in addition that can be identified and worked through as well.

I have counseled people who did not want to identify the root causes of depression because for many, it's scary what you might dig up once you start digging. I completely understand the hesitation to identify areas that may cause you to relive unpleasant and traumatic situations/events. I believe that therapy is most effective and beneficial when a person is ready, willing, and able. If an individual is not ready to deal with root causes, they should not be forced. However, they should be informed of the potential benefits of addressing and working through issues in order to have and maintain healing and wholeness, but this is an individual decision and should be respected as such.

Step 2 is about taking appropriate steps to work through the root causes. Just as each tree has its own set of roots, so do we as individuals—we have our own set of root causes. Some root causes are easier to identify than others. Most times, people think of childhood abuses and trauma—physical, sexual, and mental—such as rape or catastrophic illness and/or grief over the loss of someone dear to us. There are, however, other underlying issues that we deal with and sometimes struggle to cope with in our daily lives. I believe that one of the most significant root causes is when our expectations do not match our reality. When our life does not look the way we envisioned it, we thought we would have more money, a different job, be married, have children, live in a different neighborhood, etc. This is even more complicated when the difference between expectation and reality are out of our control. When you do everything right and things still do not line up with the plan you had in mind. When you come to the realization we all hit at some point in life, that sometimes, life just ain't fair; that sometimes, bad things happen to good people; and that sometimes, hard work does not look or feel like it is paying off.

Have you ever put something together, followed all the instructions perfectly, and the final product did not look like the picture and was imperfect despite your best efforts? Usually, we become irritated and ask ourselves who wrote the instructions or made the parts or packaged them in the box and did not notice a leg was bent or some screws were missing. Typically, the larger the item is, the higher our irritation. A wobbly toy my child is going to throw across the room and break anyway is not as important as a wobbly table my family will eat dinner at each night; and the idea of having to return it and start all over again can be infuriating. So it is when we make plans, set goals, and work toward those goals, and the reality does not effectively show our effort or progress. The larger the goal, the more disappointment we feel when that goal is not met, and the thought of starting over again seems an impossible task, especially when compared to the easier alternative of giving up.

One of the most trying consequences of this root cause is that it does not have an end. If the expectations and my reality match this year, there is no guarantee it will match next year because my expectations are always changing. We can set a goal to lose weight, and when we go to the doctor months later, we haven't lost any weight—and even worse sometimes is when we gain weight despite eating healthier and exercising. The expectation and reality of my marriage match this year, but how about next year if there is an unexpected job loss, family loss, and lack of trust to the relationship? The goals and expectations that we have for ourselves are always changing based on age, station in life, etc.; therefore, there is always the possibility that realities may not match, and the cycle of depression, sadness, worry, low self-esteem, insecurity, etc. continues in our lives.

Oh, but wait—there is hope. In John 15:5, Jesus tells us that He is the vine, and we are the branches. "He that abides in me and I in him, the same bringeth forth much fruit." *We are not alone!* Although roots go deep, we are connected to the true vine, and we can bring forth fruit in our lives and in the lives of others. We are reminded in John 16:33 that in this life, we are going to have issues when Jesus said, "These things I have spoken unto you that in me you might have peace. In the world you will have tribulation: but be of good cheer, I have overcome the world." Next, let us look at steps toward working through these root causes toward healing and wholeness.

We will look at ways to address these root causes throughout the book and to remember that there are no one-size-fits-all solutions. The first step in this process is to believe that you *can* work through these issues, and that there is healing and a wholeness just for you. Romans 12:12 says, "Rejoicing in hope; patient in tribulation; continuing instant in prayer." Remember when we asked who made this question about the product that didn't turn out correctly? Well, as Christians, we know the answer when it comes to who made us; and not only do we take comfort in that we were created by the Savior of the world, but we are encouraged by Jeremiah 29:11: "For I know the thoughts that I think toward you, saith the LORD, thoughts of peace, and not of evil, to give you an expected end."

We do not have to journey alone. One way in which you can work through these issues is with therapy, finding a counselor that you can confide in, and allow that person to help you reach your goals. Some people find a professional counselor most helpful while others may look to pastoral counselors. For some, this may also include a psychiatrist or medical personnel, who may prescribe needed medications. There are also various support groups which allow you to realize that you are not alone and to learn from others how they cope with similar situations. If there is hesitancy to talk to someone one-on-one, support groups may offer an opportunity to hear others share and only speak when or if you are comfortable. You can also attend support groups in addition to individual therapy. As a reader of this book, I believe faith may have some importance in your life, so I encourage you to consider faith-based groups if available as well.

There are three points I believe that are significant in working through these root causes. First is forgiveness, with an emphasis on self-forgiveness. Many times, we cannot progress in our journey to wholeness because of guilt, self-hatred, and obsessing about our past decisions and mistakes. It is difficult to forgive others who have harmed us or done us wrong in some way, but for some, it is easier to forgive others than to forgive ourselves. Psalm 86:5 says, "For thou, Lord, art good, and ready to forgive; and plenteous in mercy unto all them that call upon thee." 1 John 1:9 tells us that "if we confess our sins, he is faithful and just to forgive us our sins, and to cleanse us from all unrighteousness." If you struggle with self-forgiveness, ask God to help you. Ask Him to help you to believe and receive the fact that you can be a forgiven vessel, that your past can be part of your testimony of grace and mercy and not a noose that constantly hangs around your neck, and that your previous stumbling blocks are now used as stepping-stones to propel you to reach your goals and fulfill your purpose.

Second is addressing unresolved grief. We often think of grief as only being associated with the death of a loved one, but we also have to sometimes grieve the loss of hopes and dreams and grieve the gap of our life expectations and reality. For the woman who has always dreamed of being pregnant, feeling life growing within her, and then to be told that she cannot have children, although there is no loss of a person, there is definitely a loss, and that loss must be grieved. The dictionary defines grief as a 1) keen mental suffering or distress over affliction or loss; sharp sorrow; painful regret; and 2) a cause or occasion of keen distress or sorrow. Isaiah 61:3 reminds us that we can have "beauty for ashes, the oil of joy for mourning, the garment of praise for the spirit of heaviness; that we might be called trees of righteousness, the planting of the LORD, that he might be glorified."

There is comfort that can eventually come after grief. Know that it is okay to ask for help when you feel that you are drowning in unresolved grief, and the Lord will send lifeguards to stretch out their hand to catch you and pull you to peaceful ground. Identify not only people to whom you may have unresolved grief, but also things, ideas, hopes, plans, goals, expectations, places, etc. We want to experience joy where we only feel mourning and freedom in praise where we only feel heaviness.

Third is setting realistic expectations and plans to reach goals. We want to be careful not to set ourselves up for failure by setting unrealistic goals and not having specific plans to meet even realistic goals. Please do not misunderstand my statement by thinking that I am saying do not reach for the stars or set high standards for your personal goals—I am not. But I am saying that we can doubt our own progress and give up prematurely if what we set are not realistic, and we do not have specific plans. One example would be if a person who has experienced years of abuse as a child set a goal to be healed of all their trauma by tomorrow. Even if they are making great progress toward healing and wholeness, if it's not happening at the speed at which they set as a goal, they may feel they are not progressing at all, which could feed back into feelings of guilt, insecurity, self-hatred, and can potentially cause them to give up. If that same person decided to work through their issues but never make a plan on the "working" part of the process, the same cycle continues. Again, your goals may not require help from anyone in particular or your goals may require help from others; either way, set realistic goals and specific ways in which you will reach those goals.

One way to know that you are setting specific plans to reach your goal is if you can write down or verbalize the steps. For a person working toward healing from past trauma, they may set specific steps to 1) seek counseling, 2) seek support groups, 3) write letters to those who have wronged them (not necessarily letters to be mailed), 4) start a journal, etc. At any time, they can look at their steps and determine where they are in the process, what steps have yet to be started, and what steps they may have completed. When we talk about setting and reaching goals, there is nothing like a feeling of accomplishment. Constant feelings of accomplishments begin to add up to feelings of success, and our desire is that the constant successes add up to healing, and the continual healing adds up to wholeness. No team has ever won a championship without winning one game; one win after another sets you up for the prize.

The third step is to define and visualize life with reduced or no depression. As previously stated, it is important to be specific. Ask yourself, What would your daily life look like with less depression? What would your daily life look like with no depression? How will you know when you have worked through the root causes of your issues? Define it, and then visualize it for yourself. I encourage you to not only define it and visualize it but to write it down. Although the passage is lengthy, I think it is beneficial to look at Habakkuk 2:1–4.

> I will stand upon my watch, and set me upon the tower, and will watch to see what He will say unto me, and what I shall answer when I am reproved.
> And the LORD answered me, and said, Write the vision, and make it plain upon tables, that he may run that readeth it.
> For the vision is yet for an appointed time, but at the end it shall speak, and not lie: though it tarry, wait for it; because it will surely come, it will not tarry.
> Behold, his soul which is lifted up is not upright in him: but the just shall live by his faith.'

Proverbs 23:7 says that as a man thinks in his heart, so is he. Do you think you can live a life with less depression or no depression at all? Do you believe in your heart that you can work through past traumas, deal with root causes of issues, and be healed, delivered, and set free? What are you thinking in your heart? Begin to see what you want to be, don't waver, and don't give up. Write your vision on cards that you leave on your refrigerator, on your bathroom mirror, in your car, in your lunchbox, in your closet, wherever you can remind yourself of the vision you are working toward. James 1:8 says that "a double-minded man is unstable in all his ways." Do not be double-minded; be consistent in the fact that you *can* be healed and you *can* be made whole.

And step 4 is to keep your guard up. Jesus reminds us in Matthew 26:41 that we have to "watch and pray, that ye enter not into temptation: the spirit indeed is willing, but the flesh is weak." When your expectations and visions begin to match your reality, don't settle, and don't stop doing what you did to get there. You may not require continued counseling, support groups, medications, etc., but don't stop investing in you and in being the best you can be in all stages of life. If we are not careful, we can slip back into the bad habits and stinking thinking we had before we started the healing journey. If you go to a museum with fine art or an expensive jewelry store, you will see a guard, not because they just got robbed, but to decrease the risk that what they have will be taken away. Keep your guard up so that the joy, peace, happiness, self-love, and contentment that you have achieved will not be taken away, even by your own self-sabotage.

There are two scriptures that say it better than I ever could. The first is Galatians 6:9: "And let us not grow weary in well doing; for in due season we shall reap, if we faint not." You will make it if you do not give up. I strongly encourage the person who is reading this who struggles with suicidal thoughts to write this scripture down, read it, and repeat it to yourself as often as needed. Life can be so hard and so unfair, and it can be so easy to grow weary, but I plead with you to visualize a season in which you reap if you just do not give up. The second scripture is similar: "Be ye stedfast, unmoveable, always abounding in the work of the Lord, forasmuch as ye know that your labour is not in vain in the Lord" (1 Corinthians 15:58). The journey of healing is *work* (another word for work is *labor*), and at times in the process, you will feel like you are laboring full-time and overtime; but know that it is *not* in vain. Do not move from your position of self-care; do not move from your position of self-reflection; do not move from your position of self-growth; and do not move from your position in the marathon on the journey because all that labor *is not in vain*!

Now let's talk about anxiety. Although there are various types of anxiety disorders, some of the basic definitions include excessive anxiety and worry occurring more days than not for an extended period of time, finding it difficult to control the worry; the worry causes clinically significant distress or impairment in social, occupational, or other important areas of functioning. Severe anxiety can also lead to panic attacks. The four steps in dealing with anxiety are similar to those mentioned for depression, but I still think it is important to discuss it in its own context. Step one is to identify triggers to anxiety. To provide an example of a trigger, I will share my own personal experience with anxiety and panic attacks.

One autumn evening, when I was in college, I was visiting a friend at her apartment in a large apartment complex. I was walking across the grass to the parking lot to my car when I heard leaves rustling and blowing around. Then the sound of the leaves became louder, so I started looking around. And when I looked behind me, a pit bull was lunging at me. I yelled for help, attempted to fight it off as best I could, and noticed that in the shadows between two of the apartment buildings, a person was standing. Although it seemed like forever, after a short time, the person in between the buildings yelled something, and the dog ran in the direction of the person (who I assume was the owner). I ran to my car, in a panic, crying, trying to catch my breath, and steadying my hands to put the keys in the ignition.

I thank God to this day that I was not seriously injured, especially considering that I was wearing a skirt. But the dog went for my upper body, and I had on a thick coat, which had some holes in it after the incident. I was safe, was able to tell family and friends about the incident, and I continued attending my college classes. However, I had no idea of the anxiety issues I would deal with every year after this incident. Every year in the fall/winter, when leaves would fall off the trees and blow around, I would be almost paralyzed with fear, at times afraid to turn around and yet afraid not to turn around in case it was not leaves but another dog.

As we go through the steps, I will share the specifics of what I did in order to cope with this paralyzing anxiety. This is just one example of a trigger. But just as in the case of root causes of depression, there are many triggers, and sometimes, we need help in identifying those that are specific to us. Your sense of self may trigger feelings of social anxiety, past traumas may trigger anxiety issues and panic attacks, and distorted perceptions and defense mechanisms may impact anxiety. As with dealing with the unwanted tree, identifying and addressing triggers are of vital importance when dealing with anxiety. One thing you can try to consistently practice during this first step is starting and keeping a journal with the goal of helping to identify any patterns that increase anxiety or panic attacks. Do you see a pattern during certain times of the day, month, or even year, as in my case with change of season? Do certain people, places, or situations cause an increase in anxiety? Is the panic attack linked to a particular fear? Again, just because our issue may be the same, anxiety and our root causes are different and must be addressed as individual issues. However, support groups can be very helpful as you realize you are not alone in the struggle, and you can sometimes get help identifying triggers you may not have thought of on your own.

In our second step, we want to find ways to positively counteract the triggers that cause anxiety and panic attacks. The specific ways in which you counteract the triggers will depend on the root causes you identify. However, there are several verses that I believe will help all of us to begin the process and should be the foundation we stand on during this step. The first scriptures are Philippians 4:6–7 (NIV), which says, "Do not be anxious about anything, but in every situation, by prayer and petition, with thanksgiving, present your requests to God. And the peace of God, which transcends all understanding, will guard your hearts and your minds in Christ Jesus." For anyone who has experienced anxiety, that person knows that it is not a feeling that brings peace. Oddly enough, some people who experience depression have their own sense of peace, distorted as it may be, when they believe that this is the life they are meant to live or how they will always feel. Many times, it's that sense of "peace" that can lead to suicidal thoughts because they lose hope.

In general, not in all cases, the person who is depressed is striving to find hope, and the person who is always worried is striving to find peace. And yet the Word of God tells us to not be anxious about anything. The first thing that the Scripture speaks to me is that it is possible to not be worried all the time. It is possible to have a peace that even I do not fully understand. I know you are thinking the same thing I am thinking, *That's impossible.* So I will remind both of us of Luke 18:27 when Jesus said, "What is impossible with man is possible with God." If God tells me that peace is possible,

I am going to strive for peace. And the scripture that gives me some instructions of things I can do in my search for this life of peace and not continual anxiety is "prayer and petition, with thanksgiving, present your requests to God." Throughout the book, we will talk about the power of prayer.

One way in which to counteract the triggers of anxiety and panic attacks is prayer and talking to God about every single thing in our mind—every worry, every stress, every concern, *everything*. And let us not forget the "with thanksgiving" part of the instructions. Worry greatly limits our line of sight; our focus is on the person, thing, or situation that is causing the worry or anxiety. Thanksgiving takes the limits off our line of sight. Have you ever been stuck in traffic caused by construction that takes a multilane road to one lane? All you see are the orange cones, construction workers, and vehicles, which have led to the limitation of our ability to get where we are going faster and with less hassle. But doesn't it feel great when you get past that restriction, all the lanes reopen, and you can be on your way at your speed (sometimes too fast) and without hassle? To me, that is what praise and thanksgiving does.

When we adopt an attitude of gratitude, it takes the limits off my line of sight, and my focus can extend to all the good things I have going on, to the blessings I have received, and to other areas of my life where I have peace. Most importantly, it forces me to remember the goodness of the Lord and all that he has done for me. I am reminded that no problem is bigger than my God, no person is bigger than my God, no situation is bigger than my God, and nothing that I face comes as a surprise to God that he has to sit down and figure out a strategy for. He knows all—the good, the bad, and the ugly. So He knows all, and nothing catches Him off guard.

Good, bad, and ugly situations happen in my life, and yet I am reminded in Romans 8:28 that "all things work together for good to them that love God, to them who are called according to His purpose." Verse 31 asks a question that we have to ask ourselves when worry consumes us: "If God be for us, who can be against us?" I take that also to mean what can be against us—what person, place, thing, situation, and/or circumstance can have the victory in our lives if God is for us? This is another benefit of prayer. I am laying everything at the feet of the only person who has the power to change anything and everything for my good. Counteract worry with prayer and praise. I have done it in my own life, and at times, I have become so caught up in the prayer and the praise that I forget what I have been worrying about in the first place. Prayer and praise can often put you in a position to hear from God, and it is in those times that He can give answers and directions to those things that worry us and cause great anxiety.

The other scripture we want to focus on is Philippians 4:8 (NIV), which says, "Finally, brothers and sisters, whatever is true, whatever is noble, whatever is right, whatever is pure, whatever is lovely, whatever is admirable-if anything is excellent or praiseworthy-think about such things." Many books have been written, and more recently, apps have been created about the power and necessity of positive thinking. The purpose of these resources is to help people change their way of thinking because we know that perception is reality, and if we want to change a person's reality, many times, we have to begin by changing their perception.

In working through my anxiety and panic attacks after the dog situation, I learned to talk myself into a change of perception. Although my natural response was to panic about the sounds of the leaves because of the fear of being attacked by a dog, I would tell myself that the likelihood of the leaves blowing being a dog ready to attack me were slim to none. I reminded myself that leaves falling off trees was a natural part of the change of seasons, and that I can have peace during this season just as I had prior to the attack. It may seem like simple statements, but in constantly challenging my distorted perceptions that were based on fear, I was able to reestablish healthy perceptions in order to decrease the fear and change my reality. I was determined that panic attacks every fall season of every year for the rest of my life was not an option; I wanted to strive and continue to strive for peace. Please understand; I didn't snap my fingers and then stroll through the leaves like nothing ever happened. This took years of self-talk and challenging perceptions, and to be completely honest, I continue to work on these things to this day, not as often and certainly not to the level that it was years ago.

You want to challenge stinking thinking and distorted perceptions with positivity and the adjectives identified in the scripture—truth, nobility, righteousness, purity, loveliness, admirability, excellence, and praiseworthiness—without ignoring reality and creating a delusion. The fact that I told myself about the likelihood that the leaves were really a dog ready to attack does not mean that I convinced myself that it was an impossibility. I challenged my perception in order to decrease my anxiety and risk of a panic attack, but guess what? I also looked behind me if I heard a noise that was getting too close. We do not, or at least should not, constantly obsess about becoming a victim of a crime to the point that it consumes us and sends us into never-ending anxiety attacks. We still do things to protect ourselves; we are still observant of our surroundings; we have alarms in our houses and in our cars; and we may carry pepper spray or take self-defense classes. We are realistic, but we do not live with a perception that something bad always happens, and there is little or nothing we can do about it. Again, the Bible tells us to watch as well as pray.

The danger in crossing the thin line between positive thinking/changing distorted perceptions and delusional/unrealistic thinking is the risk of giving up completely. For example, if I tell myself to just get over the leaves blowing because nothing bad can ever happen and if I hear the sounds getting closer and closer (God forbid I was attacked, not by a dog but by a person), it would be very difficult to get me to think positively again and to ever challenge stinking thinking and distorted perceptions. This is why you can suggest to someone that they think about something positive, and they respond with "I have tried that before and it does not work." This person has given up completely, and every negative perception they have has turned into their negative reality. Have you ever met a person like this? That person who can find the negative in everything, to the point that you try to limit your interaction with them? Tell that person you got a good grade, and they will tell you the teacher probably graded on a curve. The weather will be nice today, and they will find a storm somewhere on the map. Or you got a raise at work, and they figure your employer is setting you up for a layoff. Challenge your perception toward the positive. And when you try and fail to think of anything positive, remember that the word of God is truth, it is noble, it is right, it is pure, it is lovely, it is admirable, it is excellent, and it is definitely praiseworthy. And so when you cannot find anything else to think on, think on those positives from Genesis to Revelations.

I will discuss steps three and four in our discussion of anxiety together. Step 3 is to look for a decrease in anxiety before complete alleviation, and step 4 is to guard against triggers. Anyone who has ever watched a child learning to walk can attest to the fact that those are small—very small steps, hence the name baby steps. Yet if the child keeps making those small steps, he/she does eventually make it to the spot they are aiming for all along. They may wobble and stumble along the way, but they get back up and restart those small baby steps again. As adults, we want to protect them from the slight bumps and stumbles, but it is in those wobbles, stumbles, and bumps where the child learns what to avoid the next time and what they have to walk around in the future in order to reach their goal.

In the same sense, when dealing with anxiety, sometimes, it is the baby steps that make the difference. Baby steps are still steps, and progress is still being made. We praise children for those baby steps, and we clap and cheer for the progress they make toward a goal. What if we become our own cheerleaders and congratulate ourselves when we make baby steps and continue to progress toward our goal? If you experience anxiety six hours a day and have at least three panic attacks a day, believe it or not, if that was decreased to five hours a day and two panic attacks, you would eventually be aware of and notice the difference.

As the child who learns what table to avoid bumping into and what to walk around instead of stumble over, you will be able to identify what possible triggers you avoid during that hour that led to a decrease in anxiety and no panic attack. What coping skills did you enact during the day in order to experience that decrease? If we can identify what you did to decrease the anxiety and panic attacks for an hour, we can begin to practice those skills more consistently until our decrease by one hour becomes a decrease by two, three, on and on until we have alleviation of constant anxiety. The same goes for triggers. What triggers, including people, places, and things, did we avoid and guard against in order to experience the decrease and how do we more consistently guard against those triggers. Remember that guarding against a trigger may not mean alleviating the trigger but changing perception about the trigger in order to change the reality that leads to anxiety and panic attacks.

It would be impossible for me to alleviate leaves from my life, so in guarding against the trigger, my focus is not on going to places where there are less leaves but instead the self-talk that assures me that leaves are not dogs waiting to pounce, they are part of nature and the changing of seasons. I guard against the trigger by being fully aware and mindful of my vulnerability while balancing my enjoyment of nature and being aware of my surroundings. In striving for healing and wholeness, I believe very strongly in the feeling of accomplishment and progress. Your baby steps matter; your learning triggers because of personal bumps, stumbles, and bruises matter, your progress matters.

Get out your pom poms, and cheer yourself on like nobody is watching. The Bible says in Psalm 85:13 that "righteousness shall go before him; and shall set us in the way of his steps." Psalm 37:23–24 reminds us that "the steps of a good man are ordered by the Lord: and he delighteth in his way. Though he fall, he shall not be utterly cast down: for the Lord upholdeth him with his hand." After a while, the child walks more easily and can run around all the obstacles that they used to run into. We can create new habits with consistency and focus. I want our testimony to be that of Proverbs 4:12 (NIV), "When you walk, your steps will not be hampered; when you run, you will not stumble."

Chapter 3

THE TRUTH ABOUT YOUR IDENTITY

When we discuss healing and wholeness, we must include the recognition of the truth about our identity. We must remember that our present position does not always reflect our divine purpose, and that the role we play does not represent everything that God has called us to be in His kingdom and in His kingdom's plans. When we think about the positions that we hold versus our divine purpose, sometimes, the position and purpose match, and sometimes, they do not. And when they do not match, we can be left feeling helpless, hopeless, and unsure of ourselves. For many individuals who have had suicidal thoughts, it is because they feel their life has no purpose. Let me remind each person reading this book that your life has a purpose! Let's look at the story of Joseph in the book of Genesis. His positions included being a visionary, who was betrayed and sold by his brothers, accused of a crime he did not commit, and thrown into prison before the realization of his divine purpose.

In Genesis 45:7–8, Joseph is speaking to his brothers, and he tells them:

> And God sent me before you to preserve you a posterity in the earth, and to save your lives by a great deliverance.
> So now it was not you that sent me hither, but God: and he hath made me a father to Pharaoh, and Lord of all his house, and a ruler throughout all the land of Egypt.

There is so much to learn from the story of Joseph. We will look at four of the lessons I learned about identity from the story of Joseph. I also encourage you to study the story for yourself so that you can receive additional revelations about your identity.

In Genesis 37, we learn about two dreams that Joseph had, which foretold of the future for him and his family. Although his sharing of the dream with his brothers caused them to hate him and, eventually, sell him, this chapter teaches me the first lesson about identity. As part of my identity, I want to be a vessel for God, and I want to be in such a position in my relationship with Him that I can be a visionary. What are your life's dreams? Are you a visionary? As we discussed in the conversation about depression, you must be able to envision yourself well. Proverbs 29:18 tells us that without vision, the people perish. So what do dreams and visions have to do with healing, wholeness, and identity? They give *hope*. When life is throwing more at you than you feel you can handle, hope is the thing we hold onto to make it through every second of every minute of every day. Many times, hope is the thin line that keeps individuals from committing suicide, keeps us in our "right minds" when we feel like we are losing the grip on sanity and stability, and gives us even minimal peace when an anxiety attack is on the horizon. Never underestimate the power of hope. Hope has to become part of our identity. Could it be hope that Joseph had as a dreamer, that allowed him to make it from the pit to the palace, despite the hell that he went through on the journey?

Life is indeed a journey—with some smooth paths, some stony paths, some mountains, valleys, swamps, twists, and turns—but if I hold onto the hope that there is a final destination that is for my good, I can make it. I may not move as fast as the others, and I may be beat up when I get there, but I can make it. Hebrews 11:1 (NIV) says it like this: "Now faith is the confidence in what we hope for and assurance about what we do not see." Our identity is associated with our testimony, and I want my testimony to be as Paul's testimony in 2 Timothy 4:7: "I have fought a good fight, I have finished my course, I have kept the faith." Pray that you can be a vessel to be used by God, even in dreams and visions. You do not have to be a prophet in order for God to give you revelations that are meant to give you hope in your future, along with your journey, and to your expected end. Let your identity represent hope that gives you the strength to fight the good fight of faith and finish your course.

A second part of identity that we learn from the story of Joseph in Chapter 39 is the importance of integrity. In this chapter, we read the story of Potiphar's wife who tried to sexually seduce Joseph, yet he refused. Due to his refusal, she lied on him, and he suffered consequences for a crime he did not commit by being sent to prison. Verse 20 tells us that while in prison, "the Lord was with him, he showed him kindness, and granted him favor in the eyes of the prison warden." Verse 23 states that "the warden paid no attention to anything under Joseph's care, because the LORD was with Joseph and gave him success in whatever he did." Of course, none of us want to be put in compromising or uncomfortable positions. Sometimes, situations arise that are out of our control, but what we can control is how we handle these situations, thus representing our integrity or lack thereof.

When we speak of wholeness, it involves both physical and spiritual wellness. We cannot be spiritually well without integrity. In Leviticus 19:2, the Lord instructed Moses to tell the children of Israel to be holy because the God they serve is holy. We cannot strive to live holy without integrity and "without holiness no one will see the Lord" (Hebrews 12:14 NIV). We cannot be perfect individuals, but we can be honest individuals, and when we live our lives honestly, we do not have to deal with the guilt and stress of keeping up a façade, which is always in jeopardy of falling and exposing the real us we try to hide from the world. We will be well, and we will be whole!

Identity lesson three is to be a person who gives to others what God has given to us when provided with the opportunity. Joseph was a dreamer and visionary; God had given him the ability to interpret dreams. While in prison, God gave Joseph the opportunity to interpret the dreams of fellow prisoners, the cupbearer and the baker, and eventually, of Pharaoh himself. Read the story in Genesis chapters 40 and 41. Genesis 41:41 tells us that after Joseph interpreted Pharaoh's dream, Pharaoh said to Joseph, "I hereby put you in charge of the whole land of Egypt." His new position not only blessed him but eventually blessed his family that had disowned him previously. Many times, when we are going through something, we find it difficult to find the time, energy, or patience to help someone else. However, often, it is in those times of helping others that we receive our blessing.

God has given each of us gifts, talents, abilities, skills, and characteristics that can help others, even while we are on our personal journey of healing and wholeness. A person who is experiencing depression can sometimes give great advice to encourage others. There is a saying that wounded people wound other people, and hurting people hurt other people. I believe it is possible for wounded people to help other wounded people as an outward expression of the empathy they have because they went through the same things themselves. Picture the soldier in a war who is wounded and sees a fellow soldier who is more wounded. Although he himself is hurt, he finds the strength and courage to help his fellow soldier. A person who experiences anxiety can still speak a word of peace to someone else. Someone reading this right now is saying "that's impossible." I remind you of Jesus's own words in Luke 18:27 that "what is impossible with man is possible with God."

Our identity must include a constant dependence on our Creator to use us for His will and to use those abilities that He has placed within us when He provides the opportunity. Another benefit of helping others is that it takes the spotlight off us and our problems if only for a short time. As I have stated before, sometimes the worse place to be is in your own head, ruminating on negative thoughts, which increases depression and anxiety. Taking a short vacation from destination *you* and traveling to destination *others* can have a profound impact on your healing and wellness. Never underestimate how much God can use you and the positive impact you can have on the life of another. On your worse day, force yourself to smile at someone. Force yourself to speak a word of encouragement and life to someone, telling them that they can make it when you are struggling to make it yourself.

We do not know the power a smile has on a fellow human being, or a kind word or a helping hand. Imagine a person who is suicidal, feeling that no one cares and no one is kind, and then they receive your smile, your kind word, your helping hand. Is that hard to imagine? Is that impossible? What if it is not? God provides opportunities throughout the day, week, and/or month for us to use the gifts he has given us, and we want to take advantage of these opportunities, if not for our own benefit, for the benefit of others. Can a person who experiences food insecurity still volunteer at a food pantry or only people who have full cabinets? Could it be that the person who struggles with sufficient food in their own homes might be the most enthusiastic volunteer at the pantry due to the compassion and empathy for those they are serving? Proverbs 18:16 (NIV) tells us that "a gift opens the way and ushers the giver into the presence of the great." KJV put it like this: "A man's gift maketh room for him, and bringeth him before great men." Use what God has given, and let *giver* be part of your identity.

The final identity lesson comes from one of my favorite scriptures in the Bible, Genesis 50:18–20. Joseph is face-to-face with his brothers, and the conversation is as follows:

> His brothers then came and threw themselves down before him. "We are your slaves," they said.
>
> But Joseph said to them, "Don't be afraid. Am I in the place of God?
>
> You intended to harm me, but God intended it for good to accomplish what

is now being done, the saving of many lives."

Our identity must include a "but God" attitude. After all that Joseph went through, his response was "but God." His forgiveness toward his brothers sets a high standard that we should all seek to follow; however, his level of forgiveness is born out of the "but God" attitude. What does "but God" attitude look like? It looks like the daily walking out of the word in Romans 8:28, "And we know that in all things God works for the good of those who love him, who are called according to his purpose." When you are running late to work, "but God"; when your schedule is thrown off track by something or someone outside of your control, "but God"; when life is hitting you hard from every direction, "but God". We do not use this attitude to hide from our reality or responsibilities but to remind ourselves that our God is greater than whatever preceded the "but God". This "but God" attitude will encourage and strengthen us when we cannot find courage or strength within ourselves. We see the perfect example of the acceptance of our reality, even in difficult times, while maintaining the "but God" part of our identity in the Apostle Paul. Paul's words in 2 Corinthians 4:8 is everyone's life testimony at some point or another. We are hard-pressed (troubled), perplexed, persecuted, and cast down; however, because of the "but God" in our life, we are not crushed (distressed), we are not in despair, we are not abandoned, and we are not destroyed. At points on the journey of healing and wholeness, we have to check our attitude. We talked about having an attitude of gratitude, but we also must have an attitude that looks adversity, trauma, brokenness, confusion, and emotional instability eyeball-to-eyeball, and we say "but God."

Although we will discuss David in chapter four, I would be remiss to have any discussion about identity and not include lessons learned from the person, who the Bible calls "a man after God's own heart." A man whose life included depression, anxiety, fear, family dysfunction, cowardice and courage, fighting and hiding, and crime (even conspiracy to murder). As with Joseph, David reminds us again that our designated position is not always our divine purpose. When we are introduced to David in the Bible in 1 Samuel 16, he has the position of a shepherd and the role of a black sheep in the family. When the prophet Samuel went to Jesse's house to anoint the next king, his father made sure all his sons were present, and David was literally an afterthought. Have you ever felt like an afterthought to those whom you should be important?

As we continue to read the story of David, we see his transformation to King of Israel and his role as part of the lineage of Jesus. Our first lesson from David is that our identity must be one that shows that we try to be the best we can be in the role that we are in at any given time. Why is this an important part of our identity? The answer is because God is still writing our story. He knows that we are in the pasture of life right now, and it seems that we are just watching sheep, doing the same thing day after day, watching what others are doing, and helping when needed. We must remind ourselves constantly that God has a divine purpose for our lives, and that we must not stop living our story. This is why preventing suicide is so important; each day gives another opportunity to live out our story and to see how God moves us from the pasture to the palace—from watching what others are doing to influencing what others are doing. Never minimize what you do and how important your story is to the Kingdom of God and the world.

I am writing a portion of this book during the coronavirus pandemic. This pandemic caused the world to shut down in many ways, yet we depended very heavily on essential personnel, and this was not only our doctors, nurses, and health care professionals, but also grocery store workers and delivery drivers. Prior to the pandemic, many people would not have thought of your local grocery store employees as essential personnel, but we learned that they truly are, and that getting through life during shut down, would not have been possible without their hard work and diligence. One of the favorite sayings I learned from my husband after we got married and after adjusting to life in the military and moving from place to place is this: "Bloom where you are planted." I encourage everyone reading this book to bloom where you are planted, and trust God to continue your story and mold your identity so you can stand firm in the knowledge of who you are and the truth of your own identity.

The second lesson we learn from David that should impact our identity is that we should use our battles as our stepping-stones. Most people are familiar with the story of David and Goliath, but that was not David's only battle. In 1 Samuel 17, when David told King Saul that he wanted to fight the Philistine (Goliath), Saul offered advice and even his own armor for David to use. In making his case to Saul, David told him of his battle with the lion and the bear. Let's review the argument David gives in verses 34–37, and how he shows us how to use our past battles as stepping-stones to our current and future victories.

> But David said to Saul, "Your servant has been keeping his father's sheep. When a lion or a bear came and carried off a sheep from the flock, I went after it, struck it

and rescued the sheep from its mouth. When it turned on me, I seized it by its hair, struck it and killed it. Your servant has killed both the lion and the bear, this uncircumcised Philistine will be like one of them, because he has defied the armies of the living God. The LORD who rescued me from the paw of the lion and the paw of the bear will rescue me from the hand of this Philistine."

Saul said to David, "Go, and the LORD be with you."

All of us face battles, whether in the past, present, or future. What if you used those battles as weapons of strength and not of weakness and as stepping-stones and not stumbling blocks? I had a personal health battle over nine years ago when I was pregnant with my first daughter. The pregnancy became high risk due to fibroid issues, DVT in leg, and pulmonary embolism. I had been experiencing shortness of breath for several weeks, and after returning home from a flight to visit my family, I remember being in the commissary on a military base we were stationed and feeling as though something had sucked all the oxygen out of the air. I found myself struggling hard to breath and looking around at other people, wondering why they were not realizing that all the oxygen had been removed from the air. For a split second, I wondered if it was some kind of a terrorist attack—an attack that would bring in suffocation to many people, yet I was the only one who was being attacked.

After being evaluated in the emergency room, it was determined that I had a DVT in my left leg and blood clot(s) in my lungs, although they could not determine how many clots in the lungs because I was twelve weeks pregnant. I was admitted to the hospital, put on an oxygen, and had an IV of blood thinner. The only thing I knew about pulmonary embolism is that it kills people. I knew this because a few years earlier, my grandmother died unexpectantly from it. My prayer in that commissary and in the hospital was "Lord, please be the air I breathe. Be the oxygen my lungs need to survive." Obviously, I was healed of the blood clots after having to endure self-administered needles twice a day and constant visits to the hematologist. So how did I use this experience as a stepping-stone and not a stumbling block. That experience gave me a new appreciation of life, and every morning, I mean it when I say, "Thank you, Lord, for this day!"

My appreciation for life does not begin and end with me. It gave me a greater appreciation for the life of my fellowmen. As a therapist, I strive to give 100 percent to the client I am helping, and I believe that they can experience happy and peaceful lives, free from constant depression and anxiety. I am not unrealistic, however, and I realize that for many reasons outside of my control, sometimes, people do not get better during my time with them, but I will have given them the best I could at the time. That experience also showed me God in a different and personal way. He was not the healer that healed those in the Bible that I read about, but He was the healer that healed *me*. When I needed air, He was the air I breathed; and when I needed peace when the fear of death permeated my every thought, He was my prince of peace. Now when battles in life arise, I remember that the same God who was those things to me then, can be those things and more to me again and again and again and again. I have had other health battles and hospitalizations, and during each of those times, I try to use the previous battle as a stepping-stone to healing and health. I share my experience, but each person has their own set of stories they can tell—their own encounters with lions, bears, and Goliaths, which means each person has lots of stepping-stones to propel them into their purpose and destiny. So *keep stepping*!

The third lesson learned from David that we must incorporate into our self-identity is having a repentant heart—be willing to repent of mistakes and call out to God in our weakness. None of us is perfect, and even despite our best attempts, we all make mistakes. Many people experience an inability to forgive themselves for past mistakes, which can be turned into feelings of depression, anxiety, overwhelming guilt, anger, and frustration; it can also lead to physical complaints, such as headache, stomach issues, increased blood pressure, and more. 1 John 1:9 tells us that "if we confess our sins, he is faithful and just and will forgive us our sins and purify us from all unrighteousness."

God does not expect perfection from us, but he does expect repentance. As mentioned before, David was not perfect; he behaved in ways many of us would never behave. If he attended church today, he would be shunned by many and talked about by all for these less than holy behaviors, yet he was a man after God's own heart. How? He was a man who was willing to repent. Look at Psalm 51 in which David is crying out to the Lord, asking that He forgive and renew Him. When we are striving for healing and wholeness, there is a renewal process that usually takes place, and we must be open and willing to allow this process to happen.

One of my favorite scriptures in the chapter is verse 12 when he asks God to "restore to me the joy of your salvation and grant me a willing spirit, to sustain me." In wholeness, we want joy, and in dealing with everything that life throws our way, we want the ability to be sustained. We discussed about identifying the roots to our problems, and in the same manner, identify your weaknesses, and call out to God from your weakness. No one is strong in every single area of life. In some seasons of life, we are strong in an area, and then the season changes, and we find ourselves weak in that same area. Don't condemn yourself or take your weakness as a character flaw that cannot be overcome.

Another important point to note is that not every limitation is a weakness. We all have gifts, talents, skills, and abilities that are unique to us, and if I am not as gifted or skilled in an area does not mean that it is a weakness. We all want what God has for us; but quite frankly, not everything is for us, and that is okay. If we are genuinely weak in an area where strength is needed, we are covered, for in 2 Corinthians 12:9, Jesus says, "My grace is sufficient for you, for my power is made perfect in weaknesses." Unfortunately, we live in a society that sometimes treats mental health issues as weaknesses to such an extent that stigmas are developed and can prohibit individuals from seeking the help they need. The strongest person in the world will require healing in some area at some point in their life, and individuals living a life of wellness is good for the society as a whole. The news shows us every day that we live within a society of many broken people. What if those individuals identified the root cause of their problems and sought the help they need to begin the journey of healing and wholeness? What would our neighborhoods, schools, churches, colleges, and world look like?

Experiencing depression, anxiety, suicidal thoughts, grief issues, and other emotional feelings are not a sign of weakness but a cry for help. If you are drowning and there are potential lifeguards all around, do you stay quiet or cry out for help? And after you receive the help and are strengthened, the Lord may use you in the future to be a lifeguard to someone else in need. God is faithful and just to forgive us, and His strength is made perfect when we are weak. So let your identity become someone that can repent of mistakes and can call out for help in your time of weakness while recognizing that not everything is a weakness or character flaw. I believe that when we incorporate these lessons into our identity, we, too, can be a man or a woman after God's own heart.

Chapter 4

THE ART OF SELF-ENCOURAGEMENT

Have you ever visited a bakery or seen elaborately decorated, cakes, cupcakes, and other forms of desserts? Many times, in looking at the baked designs, we comment that the baker has turned their job and passion into an art form. I believe we must become such experts in the area of self-encouragement that it becomes an art form. We live in a "selfie" society in which people love taking pictures of themselves and showing it to the world. Also, in this social media-based society, people love talking about and taking videos of themselves. If people are out for themselves, there may be times when no one is available to offer you encouragement. Possibly because they are busy taking "selfies."

First Samuel 30:6 (KJV) states, "And David was greatly distressed; for the people spoke of stoning him, because the soul of all the people was grieved, every man for his sons and for his daughters: but David encouraged himself in the Lord his God." Even people who have good intentions and always lend a helping hand to others in need may not have the time nor the energy to pour into us when needed. We must learn to do as David did in the midst of our despair. When we cannot find satisfaction in anyone or anything else, we must lean on the source of life and know that in the Word lies the solution to every situation, circumstance, and emotion. If David, a man after God's own heart, had to encourage himself, surely we can learn from his example.

Why does it have to become an art form? Because we live in a world in which we are constantly compared to and measured against societal norms and culture. We are encouraged to follow current fashion trends, watch the most popular shows, vote for specific political candidates based on popular policies, follow social media protocols, etc.; but we are rarely encouraged to focus building ourselves up as an independent individual in order to establish and maintain healthy mental/emotional health. Each person must become the expert on themselves and look for encouragement from inward, not outward. Colossians 1:27 (KJV) reminds us that "Christ in you, the hope of glory." John 7:38 (KJV) states, "He that believeth on me, as the scripture hath said, out of his belly shall flow rivers of living water." Get the Word in you so you are not dependent on outside influences to find encouragement.

In many ways, we have to be like the prodigal son in Luke 15:11–32. He felt he had all the answers and could handle life on his own, then in verse 17, we learn that he "came to himself," or as NIV says, "When he came to his senses." I believe there comes a point in life in which we have to get off ourselves, even in a selfie society, and admit that we don't have all the answers. Many times, we don't even have full understanding of the problems; however, we come back to our Father, who has all understanding and is able to do anything but fail. We must live out our faith in that God is *able*. When we think about getting off ourselves and coming to ourselves, we must think along the lines of John 3:30 (KJV), "He must increase but I must decrease."

I encourage you to read the story of Daniel in the lions' den in Daniel 6. In verse 10, we see that Daniel encouraged himself in prayer and worship. The verse tells us that "he kneeled upon his knees three times a day, and prayed, and gave thanks before his God, as he did aforetime." What lions' den has life thrown you into? Is it a lion's den of divorce, relationship problems, financial issues, grief, depression, anxiety, suicidal or homicidal thoughts, lack of faith, or feelings of hate or unforgiveness; the list could go on and on. Learn and practice the art of self-encouragement and have faith that not only will you be delivered from the lions' den, but like Daniel, the Lord will shut the mouths of the lion. And as in verse 23, no manner of hurt (physical, emotional, spiritual, mental, or financial) will be found on you because you believe in your God.

There are four areas that I suggest you focus on in order to begin the journey of self-encouragement. Certainly, this list is not exhaustive, and the ways in which you encourage yourself will hopefully be long, and you will add to it continuously, including inspirational books, music, church, and hobbies that highlight your passions, gift, and abilities. First, recognize, be honest about, and accept what is in and what is out of your control. To expound on this point, let us look at the story of Jehoshaphat in 2 Chronicles 20. I encourage you to read the full chapter as I will only look at a few scriptures here. Verses one and two informs us that other tribes were coming to wage war against Jehoshaphat. There are several verses I want to highlight as followed:

> Alarmed, Jehoshaphat resolved to inquire of the Lord, and he proclaimed a fast for all Judah. The people of Judah came together to seek help from the LORD; indeed, they came from every town in Judah to seek him. (2 Chronicles 20:3–4)
>
> Our God, will you not judge them? For we have no power to face this vast army that is attacking us. We do not know what to do, but our eyes are on you. (2 Chronicles 20:12)
>
> Jahaziel said, "Listen, King Jehoshaphat and all who live in Judah and Jerusalem! This is what the LORD says to you: 'Do not be afraid or discourage because of this vast army. For the battle is not yours, but God's. (2 Chronicles 20:15)
>
> You will not have to fight this battle. Take up your positions; stand firm and see the deliverance the LORD will give you, Judah and Jerusalem. Do not be afraid; do not be discouraged. Go out to face them tomorrow, and the LORD will be with you.' (2 Chronicles 20:17)

Further in the scriptures, we see that the enemies of Jehoshaphat turned on each other, and by the time

Jehoshaphat got to the battleground, his enemies were defeated and dead. So what is the lesson that we gain that help us to encourage ourselves? Jehoshaphat recognized, was honest about, and accepted what was out of his control. He knew that he was in what looked like a no-win situation, and that he needed help, not only for himself, but for his family, his friends, and his people. We fight for healing, deliverance, and wholeness, not only for ourselves, but for those we love as well. He took action on what was in his control, calling the people to fasting and praying. It is always in our control to pray and seek the face of God. When you identify what is in your control, develop a plan on what to do about it, and then act on that plan.

The attack of his enemies was out of his control, yet when he did his part, God did His part. Jehoshaphat fasted and prayed, and God delivered. Notice that God told Jehoshaphat and the children of God not to be dismayed, discouraged, or scared because they would not need to fight. However, he did not tell them exactly how the enemy was going to be defeated. Note a very important detail in the story that comes in verse 24: "When the men of Judah came to the place that overlooks the desert and looked toward the vast army, they saw only dead bodies lying on the ground; no one had escaped." If they came to the place they had to be moving, in other words, they did their part of fasting and praying, but they did not stop moving and did not bring their lives to a standstill. They kept moving, and in moving, they came to the place and was able to see their deliverance and understand why God told them they would not need to fight in the battle. Take action on those things that are in your control, and keep moving; do not stop moving. Move toward the place where you can see your healing, your deliverance, your liberty, your joy, your peace, your blessings, and, eventually, your wholeness.

Second is to approach life and the issues of life from a position of strength. Our foundation for this approach is Romans 8:31: "What, then, shall we say in response to these things? If God is for us, who can be against us?" I believe that "these things" not only refer to what the Apostle Paul was encountering but also for each of us. Imagine if when faced with an obstacle, we told ourselves, "What, then, do I say in response to this financial stressor, these relationship issues, this addiction, these hurts, these pains, these lies, these setbacks, these episodes of depression and anxiety, these ungodly thoughts, and these unholy behaviors? If God is for me, not only who, but what can be against me?"

We do not want to approach life from a defeated position. Imagine if your favorite sports team started the game with the belief that they are going to lose. What effort would be put into the game? What enjoyment would come from participating or watching the game? If you are a huge fan of any sport like myself, it is infuriating to see your team not putting forth their best effort. I have been tempted to throw many things at my television set when my favorite football team seems to bring their defeated attitude onto the field. When we have the belief that we are overcomers and that we have to ability to get through any battle, it does indeed change the way we fight. This is not to say we will not have highs and lows and bumps and bruises. In any game, the score can go up and down, with players getting injured—some mild, some major—but the game continues, the battle rages on, and this is how we must approach life and the issues of life. The great thing about this approach to life as a believer is that we do not have to feel strong or to depend on our own strength in order to assume this position. We have the perfect example of someone who tells us why.

In 2 Corinthians 12, Paul tells us about a thorn in his flesh that he pleaded with the Lord to take away three times. The answer the Lord gave to Paul is the answer the Lord gives to us as well; "My grace is sufficient for you, for my power is made perfect in weakness." When we have to take a legal oath, we are told by the leader to "repeat after me." In my spiritual eye, I can see Paul telling us the same in verses nine and ten; repeat after me:

> Therefore I will boast all the more gladly about my weaknesses, so that Christ's power may rest on me. That is why, for Christ's sake, I delight in weaknesses, in insults, in hardships, in persecutions, in difficulties. For when I am weak, then I am strong.

Third, we want to counteract those preconceived definitions that create and increase doubt, depression, anxiety, insecurity, fear, and those things that are counterintuitive to self-encouragement. Romans 12:2 instructs us to be "not conformed to the pattern of this world, but be transformed by the renewing of your mind. Then you will be able to test and approve what God's will is—his good, pleasing, and perfect will." This step goes hand in hand with identifying the root cause of a problem and the belief that is attached to that cause. Although each person will have to identify their own negative preconceived definitions and practice counteracting those definitions, I will give a few examples to demonstrate my point.

Failure is a word that typically has a negative connotation, and when we internalize this belief about ourselves, it is in direct opposition to encouragement; therefore, change the definition of what you label a failure as a learning experience. If there are areas in your life in which you would like to be stronger, then label it as an area that needs strengthening versus defining it as a weakness. When you find yourself in the midst of a dilemma, tell yourself that there are no easy solutions versus labeling it as a problem that has no options. If you are at a place of peace or contentment about a thing, instead of feeling guilty and beating yourself up because you "gave up," realize that you may have reached a point of acceptance—maybe accepting that something really is out of your control, and that is not a battle you will continue to needlessly fight.

I always encourage people to challenge black and white thinking, that something is either right or wrong; some things are simply just different—neither right nor wrong. Challenging definitions, challenges perceptions, and challenging perceptions, challenge my reality. If in fact I challenge my definition of failure, counteract it with the belief that it is a learning experience. I do not perceive myself as having failed. Therefore, my reality is not that I am a failure, which then feeds into other negative beliefs about myself and the world around me and can lead to negative behaviors that are rooted in this negative self-view and identity. We are on the journey away from self-deprecation and toward self-encouragement; transforming our mindset and preconceived definitions is a vehicle to assist with this journey.

Last, but certainly not the least, is finding and using a positive support system that will encourage you on your journey. I know it may seem odd to talk about a support system in the same context of self-encouragement, but support system is a very important and influential part of our healing journey. Proverbs 27:17 says that "as iron sharpens iron, so one person sharpens another." A good support system makes us stronger and can give us the positivity that we need to build up our courage. Each player in a game must be able to encourage themselves to do their best and fight to the finish; however, there is a reason they have pep rallies. The combination of individual encouragement and confidence, mixed with the encouragement and excitement of others, can propel us to great things—to not only win, but win big.

Proverbs 15:22 states that "plans fail for lack of counsel, but with many advisers they succeed." Never underestimate the influence of the right people saying the right thing at the right time to get your life back on the right track. It is not so important about the number of people in your support system as much as the positive influence those people have in your life. The scripture about iron sharpening iron tells me that I cannot be sharpened by someone who is not sharpened themselves. None of us are perfect, but we all know those individuals who, when we are down, help push us down further, and those who help lift us up. Our support system may consist of family, friends, church members, or complete strangers to whom we share a common bond.

When I join a Bible study, life group, women's ministry, or just spend time in fellowship with other believers, I consider it a part of my own self-care, and self-care is part of self-encouragement. Spending time with people who pour into my life in a positive, uplifting, and encouraging manner is a treat to myself. Gaining wisdom, knowledge, and understanding from a multitude of counselors is a gift you give yourself; and a gift that can keep on giving. Today, it may be you who needs the support, and tomorrow, it may be you who gives the support. People in our lives make withdrawals or make deposits; the key is balance. We do not want a support system that only withdraws and leaves us empty and drained nor do we want a support system that only makes deposits as we have to question our neediness and what we are giving in return. If someone feels they only deposit into us and have never received a return in the form of a withdrawal, they can feel unappreciated and, eventually, will decide that they no longer want to be a support at all. All relationships are about give and take, and the ability to encourage yourself helps to maintain this balance. Again, self-encouragement is a part of self-care that we have to make an art form on our healing and wholeness journey.

Chapter 5

A BRIGHT FUTURE

In our final chapter, we look at a passage of scripture that captures the essence of the importance of healing, wellness, and wholeness in the life of the believer. Matthew 5:13–16 (NIV) reads as follows:

> You are the salt of the earth. But if the salt loses its saltiness, how can it be made salty again? It is no longer good for anything, except to be thrown out and trampled underfoot.
>
> You are the light of the world. A town built on a hill cannot be hidden. Neither do people light a lamp and put it under a bowl. Instead they put it on its stand, and it gives light to everyone in the house. In the same way, let your light shine before others, that they may see your good deeds and glorify your Father in heaven.

We must strive to be that city on a hill, the salt that gives flavor to and preserves a rotting world, and the light that shines bright in the darkness around us. Each one of us is here for a purpose. God has a plan that only we can carry out during this season, and we must strive to overcome anything that would be a barrier to carrying out that plan, including paralyzing depression, anxiety, worry, stress, unforgiveness, anger, and any other mental or emotional issues that exist within us. Does wholeness equal perfection? Absolutely not, but we can live in freedom and the peace of knowing that we belong to a God who is able to help us and see His plan for our life be carried out to its fullest extent. One scripture that should be included in our self-affirmations is Galatians 2:20, which reads, "I have been crucified with Christ and I no longer live, but Christ lives in me. The life I now live in the body, I live by faith in the Son of God, who loved me and gave himself for me."

In closing, there are three lessons I want us to learn from the story of the woman at the well found in John 4:5–30. I encourage you to read the whole story as I will only focus on a few verses that I believe will summarize the previous points made in this book. Lesson one is that this woman had flaws. In today's language, we would say she had "issues." In Bible commentaries and study manuals, it is suggested that this woman was going to the well by herself in the heat of the day because she may have been ostracized by others in the community because of her "issues."

> He told her, "Go, call your husband and come back."
> "I have no husband," she replied.
> Jesus said to her, "You are right when you say you have no husband. The fact is, you have had five husbands, and

the man you now have is not your husband. What you have just said is quite true." (John 4:16–18)

Can you imagine the mental and emotional toll a woman goes through, having been married five times and currently in a relationship with another man? We may also wonder what her early life was like, what was her self-image like, and what were her perceptions and beliefs about such things as love, marriage, relationships, a woman's role, and intimacy. Did she have depression, anxiety, anger issues, or poor socialization skills? It may not be that we have had one husband after another, but that we have had one trauma after another, one loss after another, one hurt after another, one addiction after another, and so on. Similar to her, we may avoid crowds and feel ostracized by society.

That leads us to our second lesson, which is that she had an encounter with Jesus that began her healing and wholeness journey. The chapter details this conversation she had with the "man at the well" and the impact it had on her life and, eventually, the lives of others. In striving to give advice and guidance throughout the book, my primary purpose is to reassure believers that God cares, and that he is able to go on the healing journey with them and lead them to wholeness. I want each person reading this book to have an encounter with Jesus over the well of your life; you are not casting your bucket for water, but you are casting for hope, for joy, for peace, for understanding, for wisdom, for love, and for liberty. As I mentioned previously, use the resources that are available to you, including counseling, medication, etc., but please do not use those resources at the expense of that conversation.

Our final lesson is that she became salt and light because of her encounter and despite her "issues." Verses 39–42 tell us how she returned to town and encouraged others to "come see a man." She gave them her testimony, and as a result, they became believers, telling her in verse 42, "We no longer believe just because of what you said; now we have heard for ourselves and we know that this man really is the Savior of the world." What a testimony and an encouragement for each of us on our journey—the confirmation that we can be salt, spreading the flavor of the kingdom of God, as well as light in the midst of a world that seems to grow darker every hour.

We can be that city on a hill, that lighthouse for people who feel lost in an endless ocean, because our issues have become our testimony, our stumbling blocks have become our stepping ladder, our embarrassment has become our empowerment, our shame has become our shine, and our vices have become our victories. The affirmation we read in 2 Corinthians 4:7–10 is worth repeating:

> But we have this treasure in earthen vessels, that the excellency of the power may be of God, and not of us.
>
> We are troubled on every side, yet not distressed; we are perplexed, but not in despair;
>
> Persecuted, but not forsaken; cast down, but not destroyed;
>
> Always bearing about in the body the dying of the Lord Jesus, that the life also of Jesus might be made manifest in our body.

I pray that each of you share the testimony of the leper, in Luke 17, that you are healed, and as you continue to encounter Jesus, He tells you that your faith has made you *whole*.

Notes

Notes

About the Author

Ebony Hudson is a licensed clinical social worker (LCSW) who has worked in the field of social work for twenty years in various settings, including hospital, mental health, hospice, and individual therapy. She obtained her BSW from Seton Hall University and her MSW from the University of Pennsylvania. She is passionate about helping individuals live a life free of the mental and emotional bondages that limit the move of God in their lives. Her personal motto is that if she can help improve the life of one person, that person can improve their family, that family can improve their community, and that community can improve the world. She is the founder and primary therapist for EH Counseling Associates LLC, which provides biblically based counseling via telehealth. She resides in South Carolina with her husband and two daughters.

Printed in the USA
CPSIA information can be obtained
at www.ICGtesting.com
LVHW091809060924
790323LV00002B/423